Eating
Well

WAYLAND

This paperback edition published in 2012 by Wayland

Wayland
338 Euston Road
London NW1 3BH

Wayland Australia
Level 17/207 Kent Street
Sydney NSW 2000

All rights reserved
Senior Editor: Jennifer Schofield
Designer: Sophie Pelham
Digital Colour: Carl Gordon

CIP data:
 Gogerly, Liz
   Eating healthily. - (Looking after me)
   1. Food preferences - Juvenile literature 2.
   Nutrition - Juvenile literature
   I. Title
   613.2

ISBN: 978 0 7502 6813 4
Printed in China

First published in 2008
by Wayland

Wayland is a division of Hachette Children's Books,
an Hachette UK company.
www.hachette.co.uk

Looking After Me

Eating Well

Written by Liz Gogerly
Illustrated by Mike Gordon

WAYLAND

I loved staying at my friend
Ethan's house.

We ate the best snacks ever!

At tea time, Ethan's family ate the greatest grub in the world.

But, best of all, it was 'teas on knees' in front of the television.

Later, we always had a midnight feast.
But, it wasn't always fun and games.

The last time
I went to Ethan's
house, we ate
so much that
I was sick.

My stomach felt
like it was going
to explode.

I dreamed about the future, too...

When I grow up, I don't want to be unhealthy.

I want to be strong –
just like my dad.

I want to feel good...

...and have lots of energy.

Dad said that one of the secrets of staying fit and healthy is eating well.

I went to school with
a spring in my step.

At lunchtime, I ate my sandwich and yoghurt and drank some ice-cold water.

That afternoon, I whizzed through my work. My teacher was really pleased with me.

But, best of all,

I scored two
goals in our
football match!

I felt great and I wanted Ethan
to feel good about himself, too.
The secret is to eat well.

Everyone needs plenty of fresh fruit and vegetables – five a day.

Chuck the chips!

Instead, try
brown bread,

pasta, rice
and jacket
potatoes.

20

Eat fresh fish, lean meat, chicken, beans, nuts and seeds.

Cheese, yoghurt and milk are good for your bones and teeth.

Eat a balanced diet,

and you'll
be fit, healthy
and strong.

Soon, Ethan changed his ways. Now he eats healthy food nearly all the time.

But sometimes he likes a
special treat and so do I!

Now Ethan feels great!
He's taught me something
about food, too...

26

that it's fun to
grow your own
vegetables.

These days I love
good food.

I can even grow
some of my own.

I like to try new
things all the time...
Well, not quite
always, but I'm
getting better
every day.

NOTES FOR PARENTS AND TEACHERS

SUGGESTIONS FOR READING **LOOKING AFTER ME: EATING WELL** WITH CHILDREN

Eating Well is the story of two typical young boys, James and Ethan, with a healthy appetite for unhealthy food. It begins with a sleepover at Ethan's house. James is delighted that Ethan's family eats food such as chips, hamburgers and pizzas. He's also excited that they eat while they watch television – something he's possibly not allowed to do in his own home. This is a good place to stop and ask the children what they think of the kind of food that Ethan's family eats. Do they think it is healthy or unhealthy? Why is it so? What do they think about eating and watching the television at the same time? It is also a good place to discuss the importance of eating as a family. Do they ever eat at a table with the rest of their family?

The story goes on to show the consequences of the boys' unhealthy midnight feast. Again, this is a chance to discuss how eating unhealthy foods might affect people's general wellbeing. James is lucky he just feels sick because there are many worse illnesses that can be caused by eating unhealthily. The children may have examples from their own lives that they can add to the discussion.

Fortunately, as the story progresses, James and Ethan learn about eating healthily and they discover the many benefits of a balanced diet.
The story has plenty of opportunities to stop and talk about the children's own diets. What foods do they like? Do they think they eat a healthy diet? Do they know about the different food groups and what makes up a good, balanced diet? What kinds of food help people to grow strong bones and

teeth? The story also touches on eating the occasional treat. It is important that children realise that some foods are not very healthy but that it is alright to eat them in moderation.

LOOKING AFTER ME AND THE NATIONAL CURRICULUM

The Looking After Me series of books is aimed at children studying PSHE at Key Stage 1. In the section *Knowledge, Skills and Understanding: Developing a Healthy, Safer Lifestyle* of the National Curriculum, it is stated that pupils are expected to 'learn about themselves as developing individuals and as members of their communities, building on their own experiences and on the early learning goals for personal, social and emotional development'.

Children are expected to learn:
• how to make simple choices that improve their health and well-being to maintain personal hygiene;
• how some diseases spread and can be controlled;
• about the process of growing from young to old and how people's needs change;
• the names of the main parts of the body;
• that all household products, including medicines, can be harmful if not used properly;
• rules for, and ways of, keeping safe, including basic road safety, and about people who can help them to stay safe.

BOOKS TO READ

The Monster Health Book Edward Miller (Holiday House, 2006)
Oliver's Fruit Salad Vivian French (Hodder Children's Books, 1998)
Oliver's Vegetables Vivian French (Hodder Children's Books, 1995)

ACTIVITY

The Healthy Shopping Game

This is a game that tests both memory and the ability to think of healthy foods that begin with a certain letter of the alphabet. The first person to go has to select an item that begins with 'a'. He or she would say something like, 'I went to the shop and bought myself an apple.' The next person to go would think of food that starts with 'b' and say something like, 'I went to the shop and bought myself an apple and some beans'. The next person would select an item beginning with 'c' and so on.

INDEX